Growing Up, Growing In

AF624786

Dale Jacob Bockelman

BookLeaf Publishing

Presentation by *BookLeaf Publishing*

Web: www.bookleafpub.com

E-mail: info@bookleafpub.com

ISBN: 9789357211543

First edition 2023

DEDICATION

This is dedicated to my childhood self. May he live forever in me and through me; in the past, present, and future.

ACKNOWLEDGEMENT

I couldn't have done this without the love and support of the love of my life, Emily. Thank you for being my cornerstone in everything.

I also couldn't have feasibly done this if my colleague and friend Ruby hadn't introduced me to this publisher.

I also want to thank BookLeaf Publishing for letting me publish important poems to me.

PREFACE

Every poem in this book has an overarching theme of reconciling with personal childhood trauma and memories. I dove deep into existential thought. In the first couple of poems I introduce myself through simple rhyming schemes, but afterwards, it is a deep, at times, unhinged, search for my soul and exploring some of the dark corners in my mind. The second half of the book, I explore the mind of a child, and enter back into the mindset of whimsy and wonder.

Perspective is very important in these poems. I shift the perspectives multiple times, and hope this aids your further understanding of the book. In “Sinner”, I am talking directly about God, referring to God as He/Him/You. In “Salt of the Earth”, I am describing my childhood cat named Salt who passed away. Every other perspective returns to me, myself, and I. It’s a mental debate, generally between two kinds of thought (aside: it doesn’t have to be a dichotomy; it can also be seen as mutli-faceted): the wondrous child and the cynical adult. It’s a battle between preserving innocence and plummeting into a dark abyss.

I leave every word up for total interpretation for the reader. You can take the previous two paragraphs and throw it out the window and have your own interpretation of what the writing means; this is only to be used as a guide for navigating the poetry.

I tried my best for every word, every space, every punctuation mark, capitalization, every repeating word throughout each poem to hold some kind of meaning; not by mistake but by design.

I hope you enjoy, or at least take something, even if it's a fleeting thought, away from reading this.

Twenty-One

Twenty-one chisels in my soul.
In twenty-one days, that was the goal.
When you're twenty-one years in
The world wants you to grow up, not grow in.

I want to reach out and wonder,
What happened to my childhood wonder?
Is it in clear skies or thunder?
Twenty-one is just another number.

The passion, the pain, the pressure,
Can I write it in twenty-one ledgers?
Where I traded it all for pleasure.
Can its worth even be measured?

Twenty-one years, you think you're grown
Into the man you can call your own.
I thought long about the storm,
Death's been on my mind since I was born.

Here I am, in twenty-one lines,
I'm in for the fight for my soul.
The more I look, I can't seem to find
Where or what was the goal.

I hope I'm able to find my light.

Always

There will always be cat hairs in my coffee,
Always a dirty dish by my bed.
The acne scars have become a part of me,
I always thought I'd get ahead.

My glasses will always be slanted,
Coffee stains running down my teeth.
My unibrow will remain planted,
I thought it mattered more underneath.

Never knowing what to say in a room,
I always keep my opinions close.
Still waiting for my flower to bloom,
I catch my breath when posing a toast.

Our flaws will always make up
Deep down who we are,
I often get the mistakes
Mixed in with the scars.

I often think,
How lucky I can be
When I'm in a world with just you and me.

I often doubt,

If I am good enough
For the love offered when life gets too tough.

I often weep,
Drowning in my dark thoughts
When all I think is that they're all I got.

I often wonder,
Where the child has flown,
If the dream is gone,
If the child is grown.

Dark Disorders

You never seem to disappoint.
A perfect mix of chaos and order.
I often forget to pray and anoint,
As I fall back to my dark disorders.

You're a black beauty, void of perfection,
A forest hiding creatures in the night.
Not a kaleidoscopic deception,
But a clear delusion behind the light.

You were a drunk, drooling, demanding fool.
You kept playing it off like your kicks were cool.
You wear youth like armor, but it's your mask
To hide from guilt stains you thought became laughs.

You were the sins poured all over my bed,
Now a shiver from my spine to my head.
You're an animal littering the floor,
You're a tumor draped across my heart chords.

These are my dark disorders on display.
My feelings, the artist, my words, the clay.

Don’t know where they come from, but they
sure stay.
If I can only get them to behave.

Cradle The Grave

You're not good enough.
You're not fast enough.
You don't have the hunger.
You don't have the want.
You want to curl up into a little ball,
Make the world go away.
You don't want responsibility,
You act like you care but you won't act.
You hate expectations on yourself,
Yet you thrust it onto others.
You're good at self-loathing,
Became a master at it,
It's the only skill you can claim.
You want tangible things.
You want attention badly.
You want everyone to notice you, without noticing you.
You want a lasting impression on everyone you meet.
You want it all but you wouldn't know what to do,
If you had the world by your feet.

So go ahead,
Make my day.

You've said something bad.
I'll say something worse:
Stare down at the abyss,
Let it swallow you whole.
Trade the cradle for the grave.
Or Cradle The Grave, for all I care.

I'm gonna keep kicking and screaming
Soon I'll be the only voice you hear.

Keep Up

Can I catch a break?
Already caught one, but I need another.
I gotta catch up. I'm running behind.
Catch the ball, play the game,
I'll pretend it's dandy and fine.
I play myself everyday
By saying it's going to be okay.
But I'm one step away.
All it takes is one step to fall.
Stay away from the edge,
It's following me wherever I go.

Keep wasting away.
Keep it up, you'll see,
The beauty you've been bottling.
Keep up with your daily routines.
Keep up so they turn into bad habits.
Keep up with running away.
Run so far you don't know where you are,
Keep up until you're helplessly blue,
You'll see what I see in you.

Keep up with the Slow Decay
The gray suits your mood today.
You keep up because I can't anymore

Watching you waste because you were bored,
Or scared, but either way.
Soon you’ll have to face the Decay.

Keep up with slipping away,
Soon you’ll be fading away.
Keep up with keeping up,
It’ll soon be all you know.
You never had a chance to grow.

Sinner

Lord, I have sinned,
Yet I still have a grin
Slapped on my face.

Love or lust swirling,
Just another whirling
Day of angelic grace.

Too easy, too hard,
This faith is like a card,
Up my sleeve whenever I need.

I used to be God-fearing,
Yet nothing is endearing,
It's just not my type of speed.

I used to think I was safe,
I would wear You like a cape,
Now you're a faint memory.

I wept, listened, prayed,
But there wasn't a single day
When He spoke back.

Now I beat my own drum,

And the day will come,
When He's dressed in black.

Guilt and relief to me,
Is all that fills my bloodstream.

Lucid Blue

Your heart's writing checks your mind can't pay.
The straight lines you walk became circles of
gray.
A fire I thought would never stray,
Became a flicker close to blowing away.
You should have had the gasoline ready to pour.

I washed the wound I already stained.
If you're working with cupid, work on your aim.
You made your choice, now I abstain.
I lost it all, yet you had nothing to gain.
But you had everything I wanted to adore.

There's a cloud hanging over my head.
Not the kind you can see, but the kind you
dread.
I, too, bathed in a lucid blue.
Not that you wanted to ask, you never knew.
Too lost, too caught up in thinking life is a
chore.

Damn the Horizon

Somehow you're still in my head to sing.
I've let go long ago yet you still cling.
Every time I try to leave you bring
A dream I'm already living in.

I haven't thought of you in many a year,
It's not even you, it's a dream that I fear.
The dream of a promise I cannot hear.
Sometimes nothing in this life seems clear.

Sink, sink, inside the hells of time,
Where all I see is the damn horizon line.
I can’t seem to ever heed the sign,
That you're still in the rotten places of my mind.

Stolen Youth

The youth has been stolen from your eyes.
Your body isn't what it used to be.
You think it'll work, that old guise,
I shut my eyes, I refuse to see.

The body marks its visible tallies.
Scars can mark the heart and mortality.
I hide, going under the covers,
I decide to see made-up monsters.

Can you rekindle your childhood past?
Or is it lost in a sea of despair?
Do you think that love will ever last?
The glaze gets blurrier as I stare.

The glint in your eyes is gone.
In the blink of an eye, I am alone.
The child in the back of my eye has grown.

Waves Away

Can you tell me what a number means?
Does it define all of your hopes and dreams?
The days are going faster past our youth.
You slip away the second I bring proof.

You're growing up fast,
But I'm running behind.
I'll see how long this lasts
'Cause it's all in my mind.

I kept my cards close, decided not to fold.
I waited in the willows, even in the cold
I assumed we would grow silly and old.
Aging seemed alright, until I tasted the mold .

Now we're waves away, caressed by the crosshairs,
On the fringe of a feeling, we would never dare
To admit about the love that always stood there.
We both knew the curse, you didn't want to care.
Maybe I wasn't there.

Seasons

When summer sang,
We were leaves just blowing past.
When fall began,
We saw how long our love would last.

I believe in some other time,
Our leaves would have crossed paths.
But now we're out of time,
The trees alone are out of grasp.

When winter wept,
Our leaves withered in the wind.
When false spring slept,
We gambled on different sins.

When will spring sprout within our souls?
Will summer come again?
Do leaves blow in the same place twice?
Our song will never end.

I feel so cold,
Longing for summer's reason.
Becoming old,
Isn't like changing seasons.

Mirror

The man in the mirror
Is the man in my way.
He's the man I see everyday.

My sight is getting clearer,
I see the slow decay.
I decided to ignore it anyway.

"Trade the veil for the Seer"
The voice said right away.
I asked, "Won't tomorrow come today?"

"Clench all that you hold dear"
The mouth moved with dismay.
"It'll be gone when you're gray"

I laughed and gave a sneer,
"What do you know of today?
"Sit with your penance and pray"

The eyes bathed in fear.
He said, "Then enjoy today"
"Become too worried in the delay"

I saw a child draw tears,

He’d forgotten the act of play,
Shrouded in finding the next day.

The child looks through the years,
He accepts the slow decay.
He lets it define him everyday.

The man in the mirror
Is the child from yesterday.
I always knew I would slip away.

The Knife or The Noose

Last night I decided the knife or the noose,
But I just wanted to cut the rope loose.
He cried with me till we slept estranged,
But when I woke up everything had changed.

I wept, almost drowned out the room,
All I had on my mind was that Hollywood
perfume.
He didn't drag me out kicking and screaming
too,
Instead he sat in my grave and cried in my blue.

All my failsafe's fell threw the floor,
He made me walk out that door,
I wandered down a street no longer the same,
And I realized this life was no longer a game.

I could never accept your inequities,
Around me you could never feel pleased,
But last night changed everything I used to feel,
Because he believed that I could be healed.

He said, "I accept everything for who you are,"
"I accept your choices, your beauties, your scars,
"More importantly, I accept your love.

"You showed it to me everlasting from above."

He's right, I'm scared of being sad,
But a cry shouldn't be considered bad.
You said, "Repeat these words when we're blue:

"I will always love you,"

"I don't need you to give me gifts,
"I don't need your shiny silver or gold.
"All I need is for you to give me a lift
"Or warm my heart when it gets cold."

"Even among your negative thoughts,
"I know you don't mean them completely,
"You know deep down you're all you got,
"You will always be perfect to me."

"You will always be enough."

"You will find me in the meadows of your mind,
"In the horizon you thought so divine,
"And since I am feeling so inclined,
"Take these words with a rock of salt:

"It's better to build than destroy,
"Touch the ground, touch the sky,
"Feel every inch of your body, in every stretch.
"Scrub head to toe, be healthy, wealthy, and
wise,
"Have a christmas in summer,
"Reminisce of a familiar smell,
"Listen to a sound easy on the ears,

"Look for those giants in the clouds,
"Horses picking up dust to the birds in the sky,
"Find silly faces in the mountains,
"Sing a song you don't know the words to,
"Scream to a pillow, scream to the sky,
"Wear a comforting cape to go fly."

"Surround yourself in the nonsense
That makes all of the sense."

Sticky Sun

I remember the sticky sun.
I remember when we would run
Without the weight of the world.
How did it become undone?

I remember the cows and hens.
Do you really remember when,
We would stay in our own world away,
From the violence and disarray?

We created worlds from plastic things.
We discovered colors in jingle bell rings.
The sky wasn't the limit, not even space,
Nothing could contain our childhood grace.

Remember when we smiled in picnic rain,
We danced and counted droplets down a drain,
We wondered where the mushroom grows,
We counted all of our fingers and our toes.

I remember the sticky sun,
You can never take away my fun.
Because I remember the sleepy night,
And tomorrow always comes with the light.

Salt of the Earth

Your silly tongue was sticking out.
In my mind I never had a doubt.
You were so strong I was so sure.
I always thought they'd find a cure.

But then, I think again of all your adventures.
I think of your life in pain and pleasures.
I know you enjoyed every last second passed.
I knew you didn't care if you would last.

You lived life with every second to spare.
For seventeen years you lived without a care.
But then you were wayward looking for home.
You realized you didn't need to be alone.

Now your stomach is turned in knots.
I realized you think I'm all you got.
You came home looking for more than a roof.
The mark on your back was all the needed proof.

You were the salt of the Earth.
A childhood friend I held dear.
Now I hold you forever in my arms,
Now you have nothing to fear.

You are the salt of the Earth.
Sustaining, abundant, free,
You'll never know your true worth,
But you were the best boy to me.

Do What is Meaningful

Do what is meaningful, not what is expedient. Find satisfaction in your toil. Life is suffering, but working together to overcome that suffering by first and foremost - bettering yourself. Then, bettering your loved ones, therefore bettering your community will lead to an enriching life. Happiness comes as quick as it dies. It is finite. Like the Seasons changing, the springtime flowers will wither come winter. Happiness is not expedient, but an aperture for motivation to fuel the toil it takes to achieve something beyond yourself. Then you may rest and ponder on your achievements, only to get back to work and find more meaning in your life.

Wise Words From Children

What does it mean to be a kid? I asked this question to several children, from ages five to eight. The responses ranged from simple to great. It was an abstract question, it took time for the kids to come up with answers. The cogs turned in their brains, I could tell they really tried. Some kids instead asked me for a piggy-back ride.

I asked, “What do you think it means to be a kid?” A kindergartner responded, “It means… to be a kid,” I laughed while a kid started making chicken sounds. I turned around and continued with my questions.
“What’s the difference between you and me?”
“You’re old!” A small child screamed!
“You’re bigger and I’m smaller!” another said.
“But what makes us different?” I pressed.
One said, “We have more fun!”
I said she was right but she decided to run.
I asked another group of children something similar, “Do you guys think adults are just grown up kids?”
“Yes,” they answered with only one word.

I asked, “Do adults stay kids when they grow up?”
“No!” they yelled, “They turn into adults!”
“An adult has all of their grown up teeth.” said a kinder kid.
“Adults have way bigger faces,” another kid chimed in.

I moved away to talk to some older kids from grade three. I asked again, “What do you think is the difference between a kid and an adult, between you and me?”
“An adult is just a grown-up kid that’s just older than a kid.”
I pondered and wondered if this was the answer I was looking for.
Did kids really change from adults, mentally?
Do they lose a sense of being carefree?
Or can that innocence be retained?
Can it be seen as a loss or a gain?
“You’re just an older kid when you grow up,” the third-grader said.
I knew he had just hit the nail right on the head.
“But do you lose anything when you grow up?” I asked.
“You lose energy,” they said, and it felt like they shattered the glass. I was filled with amazement and wonder with the answers they told. Their

answers were so simple, so quick, when it took so long for me to unfold.

I moved back to the kinder kids, I wanted to see if they had anything else to say.
I asked the same question, but I got an interesting response, if not delayed.
"Kids play all day and adults work all day," one little girl told me.
I asked, "Can adults still play?"
"Yeah," the girl started, "But adults don't play as much as kids do,"
I don't think they knew how right they really were.

But the greatest response I reviewed, the wisest words were said from a kindergartner, words I wish I had known before. She said the difference was that kids fart more.

What Makes A Child?

Is it the loudness in their pitch?
Popsicle stains in their teeth?
Is it the dirt in their fingernails?

What if we dug deeper?

Like trees reaching for the sun,
They sprout and spread their being.
A yearning to be wild and free.

They have a vigor to learn,
Confidence in their beliefs.
Freedom in their agency.

What of their spontaneity?
Are they washed only in selfishness?
Living in the center of their universe?

What if the cradled arms break?
If the bargain was sour,
Of keeping fear at bay?

No, a child is more than these,
Their wonder is free of fears
Adults follow rules they created.

Are they fragile, little things?
Nonsense only from their tongues?
Is adulthood impending?

So, what really makes a child?
Their constant questions?
Their wandering wonder?

A child is this:
Loving all that you are
Loving your beauty, your mistakes, your scars.
Not being angry that you are sad
Or sad that you are angry
Or confused when you are not happy,
But accepting every facet of your face
Every beat you breathe,
Every mistake you make,
Every choice you create.
Being a child is accepting all that you are.
Even the scars.
Especially the scars.

Sisyphus Step

You think you need to run up that hill,
You need to push up that boulder.
You feel like nothing else is worth it,
You feel like everyone's cold shoulder.

Do you run up that hill
To be greeted by the bottom?
Do you carry that rock
Like it's your only problem?

Trade that hill for a home.
Throw the stone far away.
You were never alone,
I promise you can stay.

So what do you see?
What do you feel?
Take a moment to breathe.
You don't need to kneel.

Take a second to live,
It takes a lifetime to learn.
The more that you give,
The more life is earned.

The Choice

I will love you more based on your number.
I will always love you despite your dark
disorders.
I love you even if you cradle your grave.
I love you even if you keep up with keeping
away.
I love you because you have a sinner's heart,
I love you even if your lucid mind has fallen
apart.
I love you when you shake your fists at the
horizon.
I love you when you blame it all on stolen youth.
I love you even when you think we're far away.
I'll always be here, even in the mirror, even
yesterday.
I love you when you put down the knife and
noose.
I love when you love yourself and cut the strings
loose.
I love when you stare into that silly, sticky sun,
I love your love for animals and when they run.
I know you love wise words from children,
I know you love the cogs in a child.
I especially loved when you traded a hill for a
home.

More importantly, you love yourself.
You show it everyday, even if you don't know it.
Every new day you have made a choice
You chose life.
And that is the greatest choice.

www.ingramcontent.com/pod-product-compliance
Lightning Source LLC
Chambersburg PA
CBHW051744130826
49812CB00033B/995
* 9 7 8 9 3 5 7 2 1 1 5 4 3 *